More Fun Ideas for
Advancing Modern Foreign Languages

in the Primary Classroom

Sue Cave

Brill
PUBL

We hope you and your pupils enjoy the activities in this book. Brilliant Publications publishes many other books for teaching modern foreign languages. To find out more details on any of the titles listed below, please log onto our website: www.brilliantpublications.co.uk.

French Festivals and Traditions	978-1-905780-44-0
Bonne Idée	978-1-905780-62-4
¡Es Español!	978-1-903853-64-1
Juguemos Todos Juntos	978-1-903853-95-5
¡Vamos a Cantar!	978-1-905780-13-6
Spanish Pen Pals Made Easy	978-1-905780-42-3
Lotto en Español	978-1-905780-47-1
Spanish Festivals and Traditions	978-1-905780-53-2
Buena Idea	978-1-905789-63-1
Das ist Deutsch	978-1-905780-15-0
Wir Spielen Zusammen	978-1-903853-97-9
German Pen Pals Made Easy	978-1-905780-43-3
Deutsch-Lotto	978-1-905780-46-4
German Festivals and Traditions	978-1-905780-52-5
Gute Idee	978-1-905780-65-5
Giochiamo Tutti Insieme	978-1-903853-96-2
Lotto in Italiano	978-1-905780-48-8
Buon'Idea	978-1-905780-64-8

100+ Fun Ideas for Practising Modern Foreign Languages in the Primary Classroom	978-1-903853-98-6
Chantez Plus Fort!	978-1-903853-37-5
Hexagonie 1	978-1-905780-59-4
Hexagonie 2	978-1-905780-18-1
Jouons Tous Ensemble	978-1-903853-81-8
C'est Français!	978-1-903853-02-3
J'aime Chanter!	978-1-905780-11-2
J'aime Parler!	978-1-905780-12-9
French Pen Pals Made Easy	978-1-905780-10-5
Loto Français	978-1-905780-45-7

Written by Sue Cave
Illustrated by Kate Taylor
Photos by Reeve Photography Ltd.
Editorial, design and production by Hart McLeod Ltd.
Front cover designed by Brilliant Publications

A special thanks to the pupils and teachers at Radstock Primary School for allowing us to take the photographs used in this book.

Printed ISBN: 978-1-905780-72-3
ebook ISBN: 978-0-85747-003-4

First printed and published in the UK in 2010

Published by Brilliant Publications
Unit 10
Sparrow Hall Farm
Edlesborough
Dunstable
Bedfordshire
LU6 2ES, UK

E-mail: info@brilliantpublications.co.uk
Website: www.brilliantpublications.co.uk
Tel: 01525 222292

Contents

Language learning tools   9

Language learning strategies   9

Knowledge about language   20

Advancing oracy and literacy skills

Manipulating and reusing more complex language

Reading and decoding unfamiliar language 65

Presentation, creativity and performance 71

Preface

This resource book is designed to complement *100+ Fun Ideas for Practising Modern Foreign Languages in the Primary Classroom*, which are appropriate for young learners in their initial stages of learning a modern foreign language.

The ideas in this book are designed to provide practice in using and understanding more complex language. By learning how to manipulate and decode language, recognizing how language can be learnt and practised, as well as how this newly-learnt language functions at sentence level, the pupils will realize that languages can be mastered and this is empowering. The activities in this book enable creative communication and will give young learners a feeling of ownership of the language being learnt.

All these activities can be used to work towards the Year 5 or Year 6 objectives in the 'Key Stage 2 Framework for Language Objectives' (see page 8). They are suitable for most languages and for a wide range of topics. The resources required to set up most of the activities are those found in the primary classroom.

In line with the previous title for younger learners, the key ingredients of manipulation, competition, surprise, movement and secrecy are also inherent in these activities. However, the additional ingredients of challenge and purpose are emphasised.

These are not all my original ideas but ones which have been tried, tested and adapted in my teaching in the primary classroom. I hope that they contribute to both your own enjoyment and the enjoyment of your learners, as they develop their ability to be more confident and proficient speakers of another language.

Sue Cave
April 2009

Team games and competition

Some of the activities in this book suggest how a competitive element can be used. I have found that competition encourages children to participate more readily and with even greater enthusiasm than they might do otherwise. Children who seem to be reticent, or appear to lack confidence in using a foreign language in the classroom, often relish the opportunity to join in with a competitive game. This seems to be true for many boys in particular. Team games remove the emphasis on the individual and allow children to learn, perform and develop skills within the 'safety' of a group of peers.

I avoid single sex teams but try to orchestrate teams that include a range of abilities. These teams are normally organized during a teaching session, with new ones formed in the next lesson. However, you could keep the same teams and develop a 'league' to which points are added after each game.

As in any competition, rules are essential to ensure the smooth running and fairness of the game. I tell the children that the teacher is the referee and that the 'ref's' decision is final! I allow the winning team to perform a victory salute and announce, in the target language, that they are the champions. This is a privilege given only to the winners, which becomes respected and esteemed by all.

Team games are always popular. The children become so engrossed that they are oblivious to the amount of practice and repetition taking place. You might guess from this that I like team games and find them an effective strategy in language learning. However, if you feel that it would be more appropriate for your class to learn in a less competitive atmosphere, most activities can be played just as well without explicit competition.

Links to Key Stage 2 Framework for Language Objectives

Language learning strategies
Activities 1–11

Knowledge about language
Activities 12–35

Objective	Activity number
O5.1	2, 36, 37, 40, 41, 67
O5.2	39
O5.3	2, 38, 42, 43, 44, 48, 49, 51, 57, 58, 59, 60
O5.4	48, 71
L5.1	43, 44, 48, 54, 56, 59, 60, 65, 67
L5.2	45, 46, 47, 48, 49, 50, 60, 65
L5.3	47, 48, 49, 51, 54, 60
O6.1	66, 73
O6.2	70, 71, 73, 76
O6.3	43, 68
O6.4	57, 68, 69, 71, 77
L6.1	63, 64, 68, 75
L6.2	16, 62
L6.3	43, 64
L6.4	70, 72, 73, 74, 75, 76

Language learning tools

Language learning strategies

It is important that children are aware of how they learn a language. To achieve this, frequent classroom discussion is essential and becomes an integral and valued part of every language lesson. Very quickly and without prompting, children share their learning strategies. Whether memorizing and recalling language, decoding meaning, recognizing patterns or applying prior knowledge, their ideas are often inventive, creative and occasionally surprising.

The following activities are designed to provoke discussion about language learning. The language in question could be the child's first language, the target language or even a language unfamiliar to them.

Activity 3, 'Chinese whispers'

1.   Language detective notebook

✦   'Detective training' page – encourage children to write down, in a notebook or something similar, strategies to memorize and practise language which work for them.

✦   'Clues' page – children can make a list of ways to predict meaning and understanding based on prior knowledge, context, tone of voice and gesture.

✦   'Detective rules' page – this will include information about how the language is constructed.

✦   'Detective procedure' page – this will detail how to plan and prepare for a language task, as well as how to practise new language.

✦   'Detective code' page – this could contain information about the sounds certain letters make and the best ways to communicate with someone.

✦   'Detective's reference' page – here children can keep reminders about how to use a bi-lingual dictionary, for instance.

✦   Encourage them to be 'language detectives' at all times by writing down the strategies that work for them.

2.   Mime a sentence

Use this activity to discuss the importance of gesture in communication.

✦   This is like charades, so it may be necessary to agree at the start actions for 'first word', 'second word' etc, as well as a mime for definite and indefinite articles.

✦   Whisper a sentence, or give one on a card, to a pupil to mime.

✦   The others in the group must try to identify the exact sentence by observing the actions of their classmate.

✦   This game is made easier if the sentences being mimed are ones which are familiar to the class, which therefore limits your choice. However, to illustrate the importance of gesture, try using familiar language in unfamiliar constructions.

✦   The children could devise their own sentences.

3.   Chinese whispers

✦   Arrange the pupils in lines of about six to eight children.

✦   Whisper an unfamiliar word or sentence to the first child in the line and say that this must be whispered down the line facing away from the person with whom they are communicating.

✦   Ask the last child in each line to say aloud what they were whispered and see if the result is close to the original.

✦   Repeat the activity, but this time tell the children that they should face each other as the word is whispered.

✦   Once again, compare the final words with the original.

✦   Hopefully, the children will find that when they can see the face of the communicator, it is easier to repeat what is being said.

✦   Use this activity to discuss the importance of being able to see the shape of a person's mouth when learning a new language.

✦   This activity could be repeated a third time, allowing for as much repetition of the whispered phrase as is needed, to reinforce this strategy.

4. Memory game

✦ Present some unfamiliar objects on a tray, or as images on the whiteboard.

✦ Tell the children that they have a limited amount of time in which they can ask to hear the word in the target language. This works well with languages that are totally unfamiliar to them.

✦ The children may ask for repetition of the words as many times as they want within the allotted time.

✦ When this time is up, they must try to recall as many words as they can.

✦ Ask the children to share their methods of recalling the unfamiliar language and discuss how these can be used when learning the new target language. The ideas will undoubtedly be varied and interesting!

5.   Make the link

This activity identifies the importance, when learning a language, of prior knowledge.

✦   Choose some words in the first language of the classroom, which are largely unfamiliar to the class. Make sure they have connections with words in either the target language being studied, or other areas of the curriculum. These links should help the children to decode the meaning of the unfamiliar word, eg if the children know the word 'sept' from the French word for seven, they may be able to deduce the meaning of septuagenarian – a person in their seventies.

✦   Provide also a list of images that correspond to each unfamiliar word.

✦   In groups, ask the children to match the words to the correct image.

✦   Afterwards, discuss how they decided on the meaning of the words and how prior knowledge helped them.

6.   Full stop or question mark?

Children seem to really enjoy doing this activity. It helps to focus on the importance of intonation in decoding language.

✦   In some languages, a difference between the intonation of a statement and a question is evident.

✦   Say aloud sentences that are either statements or questions.

✦   Ask the children to indicate after each statement what type of sentence they think it is, by either drawing a question mark in the air or punching the air with their finger to make an imaginary full stop.

Using dictionaries

The distribution of bi-lingual dictionaries in a classroom often seems to cause a frisson of excitement. This is probably because they give access to a wide range of vocabulary not previously encountered. However, dictionaries have limited value unless the young learner knows how to use them. Important dictionary skills include:

✦ locating words

✦ understanding abbreviations and their relation to word classes

✦ understanding the sound system of the language in order to pronounce words both individually and in a sentence.

Access to dictionaries designed for young learners is also essential as these are invariably shorter and simpler. Also, depending on the age and ability of the child, a review of alphabetical order is often necessary before using a dictionary to locate a word. The following exercises can help with this.

---

7.   Alphabetical order

✦ Ask small groups of children to organize themselves in a line in alphabetical order according to the first letter of their name.

✦ Once they are confident in doing this, combine groups and ask them to reorder themselves until the whole class is in alphabetical order.

8. Human alphabet

✦ Make a set of word cards in the target language.

✦ Distribute the cards, giving one to each child.

✦ Ask the children to organize themselves in a line so that the cards are in alphabetical order.

✦ This could be made competitive if the children are in groups, by timing them to see which is the fastest.

9.   Musical alphabet

✦   Place the word cards from activity 8, 'Human alphabet', in a feely bag and play some music. When the music stops, a child takes out a word card and stands up.

✦   Play the music again. When it stops, the next child takes out a card and stands next to the first according to alphabet order, normally left to right, depending on the language.

✦   The game continues until all the words are out of the bag.

10.   Alphabet knockout

This activity is ideal if used after activity 8, 'Human alphabet', or activity 9, 'Musical alphabet'.

✦   Use the cards from the previous activities. Once the children are in an alphabetical line, distribute some different word cards to other children.

✦   Each child looks at their word and takes it in turn to replace or 'knockout' a child in the line with their new word, ensuring they are in the correct place alphabetically.

Once the children become more familiar with the order of the alphabet, the next stage is to locate a word in the target language and then find its meaning in the children's first language.

I avoid games that involve a race to find a given word first, as this can be rather disheartening for those who are slower. Working in pairs to practise locating words at a leisurely pace results in greater confidence. Then, team games such as activity 11, 'Scavenger hunt', can be played.

11. Scavenger hunt

This team game gives practice in using a dictionary to find the meanings of words.

✦   Give each group of children bi-lingual dictionaries and a list of items in the target language to be found within the classroom. This can also, if appropriate, include items outside the classroom.

✦   The winning group is the one who locates and presents all the items on the list.

✦   If the list includes a definite or indefinite article, discussion is needed first about what is the first letter they will look up.

Using a dictionary to speak or write in the target language will come later. First, it is important that pupils have a better understanding of the structure of the language and its pronunciation.

Knowledge about language

In addition to strategies for learning language, an understanding of how and why a sentence is constructed in a particular way, as well as how the words in a sentence are pronounced, are basic language learning skills. The following activities allow practice of this.

Activity 22, 'Agreement scrabble'

Word classes

Many children seem to find the connection between the name of a word class and its concept difficult. They can often name the different classes of words but can't remember their functions.

12. Word class actions

Devise actions for nouns, verbs, adjectives, adverbs, conjunctions. For example:

◆ For a noun, place a hand above the eyes as though looking in the distance. I explain that this is the action for a noun as everything they can see is a noun.

◆ For an adjective, I continue to hold my hand above my eyes, whilst wriggling my other hand at the side of my head, thereby making the noun more 'interesting'.

◆ To demonstrate a verb, you might move on the spot. An adverb is moving on the spot but 'strangely'. This one is always an appealing action!

◆ For a conjunction, link together the first finger on each hand to indicate that two parts are being connected.

It doesn't really matter which actions you employ as long as you are consistent. This kinaesthetic approach to word classes seems to be effective for many pupils.

13.   Word class calling

✦   To familiarize children with the word class actions and to practise their meanings, call out a word class and ask the pupils to respond by performing the action.

✦   Ask for examples of words from different categories in the target language and make a list of them for all to see.

✦   Call out words in the target language from the agreed list and allocate a point to the first child who does the correct action. After a while, and if appropriate for your group of learners, remove the list of words from sight.

✦   The child with the most points wins and can then be the caller if they wish.

14.   Word class movement

✦   Discuss the abbreviated forms of word classes as found in dictionaries, eg n for noun, adj for adjective.

✦   Display a sequence of these abbreviations on a whiteboard, eg n, n, vb, adj.

✦   Call out the word classes in the sequence of the displayed abbreviations: noun, noun, verb, adjective.

✦   Ask the children to perform the agreed actions for each word class as you call them out.

✦   Once familiar with the actions and the sequence, play a piece of music to accompany the movements. If possible, choose music in which the syllables of each word class fit the beat.

✦ If you choose a catchy piece of music, you will find the children continue to sing the word class sequences after the activity is finished.

15. Simon says word classes

This game is always a favourite.

✦ Call out word classes with the prefix 'Simon says'. The children must then perform the relevant actions unless 'Simon' doesn't say so. Anyone doing the action if 'Simon' hasn't told them to is out.

✦ Make the game a little more challenging by calling out words in the target language instead of the word class.

16. Foreign language detectives

◆ If you have access to bi-lingual copies of well-known storybooks, choose one in a language unfamiliar to the children.

◆ Ask the children to identify words from different categories and justify their reasoning.

◆ Each correct answer earns them a letter clue. The letter clues form an anagram of the language in which it is written.

Word cards

The following activities require sets of word cards to be made. Although a little time consuming to make, consider them as an investment, as they can be used for a variety of games as described below.

---

17. Word class happy families

Play this game once the children are familiar with a series of sentences from a given topic in the target language.

◆ Print out the sentences on card and cut them up into words. Make enough sets so that the class can play in groups of about six.

◆ Ask the children to distribute about half of the cards to their group, so that each child has a few cards in their hand. Place the rest in the middle of the table.

◆ Each child takes it in turn to ask someone in their group if they have either a verb, noun etc depending on the types of sentence being practised.

✦ Once a child has four cards of a particular word class, they have a set and must turn the cards upside down.

✦ If the person who has been asked for a card does not have one of that word class, the child asking takes a card from the central pile and misses a go.

✦ The winner is the child with the most sets once all the cards have been collected.

18. Sentence word class happy families

This is like the previous game, except this time the children must collect individual verbs, nouns, adjectives etc in order to form a sentence.

◆ They take it in turns to ask someone else in their group if they have a particular word type. If they do, they hand it over.

◆ When a child has the necessary words to make a sentence, the cards are placed down before them and count as a set.

◆ The child who makes the most sentences, once the cards have all been used, is the winner.

19. Word class lift and show

Once again, use the sets of cards as in the previous activities and put the class into teams.

✦   Call out a word class, eg verb.

✦   The first team to lift and show a word card with a verb on it, wins a point.

20. Word class groupings

Use the same cards as in the previous games but include cards containing word class headings, such as 'verbs', 'adjectives' etc and group them into these categories.

✦   Split the class into teams and give a set of cards to each team.

✦   Ask the children to group the cards under the different word class headings.

✦   The first team to correctly group the cards is the winner.

Language rules

Each language has its own rules regarding how sentences are constructed. It is important for children to be familiar with these rules, such as word order, use of articles and how verbs and adjectives change, so they can apply this knowledge to build and understand sentences.

---

21. Be negative

✦   Choose about 25 simple negative sentences that have a noun, verb and negative word or words. Make a set of cards. On each card write one word from the sentences.

✦   Arrange groups of about six children and ask them to distribute the cards so that each child has six. The remaining cards should be placed in a pile in the centre of the table.

✦   Each child takes it in turn to put down a card, if they can, to build a negative sentence. If s/he has not got a suitable card to put down, the turn is missed and another card is taken.

✦   When the last word of a sentence is put down, the cards are removed and a new sentence is started. The child who put down the last word puts down a card to start a new sentence.

✦   The winner of the game will be the first child to get rid of all the cards in their hand.

22. Agreement scrabble

This is quite a challenging game so keep the sentences simple.

✦ Using sentences with familiar vocabulary, make sets of cards with a word from the sentences on each card.

✦ Make sure you use a variety of sentences with different verb endings or adjectival endings, as appropriate.

✦ Ask the children to distribute the cards equally, making sure some remain in the centre. How many cards each player has will depend on the total number of cards and pupils in the group.

✦ Tell the children to take it in turns to put down a card in order to create a sentence in which the agreement is correct.

✦ If a child cannot go, s/he picks up another card and misses a go.

✦ The first child to get rid of all his/her cards is the winner.

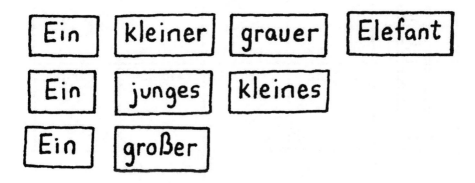

23. Verbs snakes and ladders

✦ Create a simple snakes and ladders board with verbs showing different endings in each square. You should be able to find a template by searching on the Internet.

✦ Customize blank dice with pronouns in the target language, eg he, she, they etc.

✦ Each child takes it in turn to roll a die, before moving their counter to the nearest square containing a verb that corresponds to the pronoun shown on the die.

✦ Snakes and ladders rules apply.

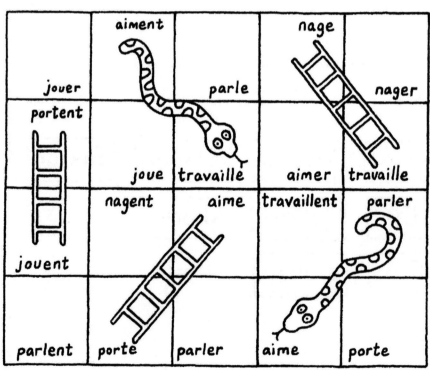

24. Verb pairs

✦ Hide verbs with different endings and pronouns behind numbered cards or shapes on the interactive whiteboard.

✦ Divide the class into two teams.

✦ Each team takes it in turn to choose two cards. If the verb ending agrees with the pronoun, the pair is taken away and the team wins a point. If they do not, they are turned back over.

✦ The team with most pairs at the end wins.

This game could also be played to match nouns and adjectives as well as singular and plural nouns. In fact, any words that need to agree.

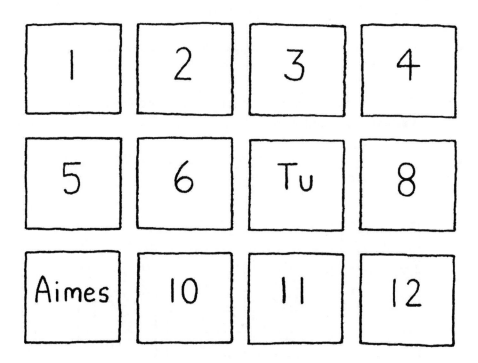

Phonics and pronunciation

To be able to use a dictionary to create a sentence and say it aloud, children need to be able to recognize and vocalize the sound of letter strings that are different to those of their first language.

---

25. Sound, action, spelling

✦ Ask the children of what a particular sound in the target language reminds them and agree on this as a class. It is best to ask the children, rather than choosing the sounds yourself, as new learners often have very different perceptions of language sounds.

✦ Agree on an action that matches their perception of the sound. Then find a suitable image to accompany the action.

✦ Create flashcards of the images with the accompanying grapheme(s) for a particular phoneme.

✦ Every time the sound is encountered during lessons, use the flashcards as reinforcement.

✦ If possible, create a phonics image frieze for the classroom wall and refer to it constantly.

| oi | ou | u | o/au |

26. Singing phonemes

✦ Create grapheme cards for a selection of sounds. Allocate one sound card to a group of several children.

✦ Conduct the 'phonic orchestra' by pointing to a group who produce the sound in unison. Like a conductor, indicate whether you want them to say it loudly, quietly, quickly or slowly.

✦ Once they become familiar with these sounds, conduct the whole class by pointing to the graphemes on a whiteboard and singing the phonemes to a well-known tune or nursery rhyme. Confident children could take turns at being the conductor.

27. Phonic bingo

Bingo is always a popular activity, regardless of the content.

✦   Just like number or word bingo, children write a selection of graphemes on a mini-whiteboard or piece of paper.

✦   You call out the sounds and the first child to cross off all their selection correctly must shout out either 'bingo' or 'lotto' as appropriate. They are then the winner.

28. Phonic rap

✦   In groups, children choose a few sounds in the target language which they enjoy making.

✦   Ask them to work as a group to create a pleasing sound sequence using the phonemes they've chosen.

✦   Encourage the use of either the agreed actions for the phonemes, or their own to accompany the sequence.

✦   Invite each group to perform their sequence and the rest of the class to identify the sounds.

29.   Guess the word

This is a good way of focussing on the mouth shape needed for an unfamiliar sound.

✦   Using familiar vocabulary, sound out a word by saying aloud the letters common to both the first language and the target language.

✦   Mime the other phonemes with the agreed action, mouthing the sound at the same time. Ask the children to try and be the first to guess the word.

30. Splat the grapheme!

Try playing this game in pairs.

✦ Give each pair a sheet of paper with graphemes printed on it.

✦ Call out a sound. The first child to splat the correct grapheme wins a point. 'Splat' involves slapping down a hand on the correct letters.

✦ Alternatively, call out a word. The first child to splat a grapheme found in that word wins a point.

✦ Consider laminating the sheets, as paper may not be able to withstand the force with which hands are enthusiastically slapped down!

31. Songs, rhymes and phonic actions

✦ Play a familiar song or rhyme in the target language and ask the children to focus on one or two repetitive phonemes in it.

✦ Each time the sound is heard, a bean bag or bags can be circulated around the class.

✦ A more amusing version of this game involves the pupils, when the chosen sound is heard, performing the agreed phonic action.

32. Phonic hangman

This is like the traditional game of hangman, but instead of a line representing a letter, in this version it represents a sound. This can be one letter or several depending on the sound.

✦ Display lines indicating the missing letters in a word. The children then suggest a phonic sound and the hangman game proceeds as usual.

✦ To make the game more challenging, as well as suggesting the sound, the children could be asked to name the letter(s) that make the sound.

33. Throw the phoneme

This activity is suitable for words that can be represented by soft objects such as toy animals, coloured bean bags, bean bags with numbers on them, items of clothing or possibly plastic foods.

✦ Arrange the children so they are sitting in a circle, before distributing the items.

✦ Call out a phoneme. If a child believes that s/he is holding an item that contains that sound, they toss the item into the centre of the circle. There is something very satisfying about tossing the items!

✦ However, if you think this game may get out of hand owing to over-enthusiastic throwing, ask the children holding an object with the relevant sound in it to stand up and swap places with another child who has done the same.

✦ It is important to ensure that either there are several items that contain the same sounds, or that some items are duplicated.

34. Mexican wave consonants

✦ Arrange the children in a circle. The best way to do this is to tell them to stand close to the four walls of the classroom.

✦ Check they understand the concept of a Mexican wave.

✦ Allocate a consonant to each child – use several.

✦ Choose a new sound to practise and call it out. The children perform a Mexican wave by saying their consonant followed by the chosen sound as they raise their arms in the air. This can make a pleasing sound if the wave flows well!

35. Phoneme fruit salad

✦ Arrange the children in a circle, either on chairs or seated on the floor.

✦ Choose a selection of new sounds and give one to each child. Ensure that several children in the circle are listening for the same sound.

✦ Call out one of the sounds. At this point, all children who were given that sound stand up and change places with each other.

✦ To make the game more interesting, suggest different ways each time for how the children should move to their new place. For example, like a particular animal or adverb. Alternatively, ask them to call out the sound repeatedly until they arrive at their destination. This can be very noisy, but enjoyable!

✦ Occasionally, call out the phrase 'fruit salad' in the target language. At this point all children must stand up and change places.

Advancing oracy and literacy skills

The following activities are grouped into three broad areas of development. These relate to the oracy and literacy objectives for Years 5 and 6 in the Key Stage 2 Framework for Languages. What distinguishes these activities from those for beginners is that the language being practised is more complex.

Manipulating and reusing more complex language

To be able to create sentences of their own, children first need lots of practice in manipulating language. This allows them to explore how it fits together. With mastery of phoneme and grapheme links, new language can be quickly incorporated into sentences in both oral and written work. This removes the need to practise these skills separately.

Reading and decoding unfamiliar language

In order to decode language in unfamiliar texts, the children will need to have a good grasp of the sentence structure and rules of the foreign language. A reminder of strategies for predicting meaning through the application of prior knowledge and context clues will also prove helpful.

Presentation, creativity and performance

In many ways, the final activities of this section are the ultimate goal, namely to understand unfamiliar language and produce language of one's own choice in order to communicate. The pupils' first attempts may be hesitant and inaccurate but the decoding, as well as creation of a first sentence, will be memorable both for learner and teacher.

To participate in many of the activities, it will be necessary to use reference material or a dictionary. If the children have not had much practice in using dictionaries, perhaps some of the activities in 'Language learning strategies' at the start of this book could be used first. An understanding of the function of word classes, their abbreviations and their role in the sentence structure of the target language will be essential in order to select the correct word from a dictionary. In addition, a good understanding of grapheme and phoneme links will be necessary in order to read aloud and share any language which is created.

Activity 43, 'Pictionary'

Manipulating and reusing more complex language

The following activities can be used to practise a wide range of topics. Their purpose is to develop language learning skills rather than teach specific content. If you are free to choose the vocabulary to be taught, consider language that will primarily develop phonic knowledge and an understanding of language structure. Children particularly seem to enjoy creating sentences that are silly or nonsensical. They create humour which can be shared and this in turn makes it purposeful. They will need little encouragement in creating sentences of this nature.

Many of these activities require sets of cards to be made. If time and resources are in short supply, most of them can be created on an interactive whiteboard. The interactive 'dice' feature, or anything similar that can randomly generate a selection of words that you have entered, provides additional possibilities for the selection and manipulation of language. The only disadvantage to using an interactive whiteboard is that not as many children will be actively involved at any one time.

Activity 41, 'Pause and say'

36. Human fruit machine

This activity requires large foam cubes with plastic pockets. They are not very expensive to purchase and can be used time and again. You may find some in the infant section of your primary school.

◆ Insert images into the plastic pockets, which represent different parts of the complex sentence being practised. For example, one die will have images for the noun in the sentence, another for the verb. A variety of images on each of the six sides is more interesting.

◆ Ask children to come to the front of the class and hold a cube. Explain that they will become part of a human fruit machine. You will never be short of volunteers!

◆ The children arrange themselves in the order of the sentence structure.

◆ On the count of three, each child chooses a side to show to the class, who then read out the randomly generated sentence. A nonsensical sentence will often be created, but this is the appeal.

37.   Guess the sentence

✦   An alternative to the previous activity is that each child selects a side of the die but does not show what it is, by standing with their back to the rest of the class.

✦   This can then be played as a team game. Split the class into teams. A person from each team makes a guess at the sentence being hidden.

✦   If a part is guessed correctly, the child turns around and the side of the die is shown. The teams take it in turns to guess.

✦   The winning team is the one to guess the exact sentence.

38.   Answer the question

This is quite a challenging game as the classmates don't know which question will be asked and have to respond appropriately. It requires them to listen attentively.

✦   Select four or five questions in the target language with which the children are familiar, eg 'Do you like mushrooms?' or 'What is today's date?'

✦   Each question is allocated to one child. These four or five children then leave the room.

✦   Ask the rest of class to put their hands under their desks. One child will be given a soft toy to hold but everyone will pretend to be the one concealing it.

✦   Invite the questioners to return to the classroom and ask their question to fellow pupils. Their classmates respond to the question posed to them in the target language.

✦   However, the child who is concealing the soft toy responds

45

to the question asked before promptly pulling the toy out from its hiding place. It is only when the complete response is given that the questioner will know if the toy has been located.

✦   The winner is the first questioner to locate the soft toy.

39. Find someone who likes...

This activity is to practise expressing opinions.

✦   Give each child a sentence that states something liked and disliked. Each sentence must be duplicated, so that each child's sentence matches another.

✦   The children must ask each child in their class what they like. They respond by saying what they like and what they dislike according to the statements given.

✦   If the responses are exactly the same as the statement given to them, they sit down and stop asking questions.

✦   The activity continues until everyone has found their partner.

✦   An alternative to this is to give each child a list of objects, eg types of food. The children must then find and note down a different person in the room who likes and dislikes each item.

40. Full stop and out!

Play this game in small groups rather than as a whole class to avoid each child having to wait too long for their turn.

✦   Ask each child to say, aloud and in turn, a word to create a sentence.

✦   The word given must be in correct grammatical order according to the target language.

✦   If a child is no longer able to provide a word to lengthen the sentence, they must say 'full stop and out!'

✦   The child who cannot lengthen the sentence is out in the next round. The game continues until there is a winner.

41. Pause and say

This is a 'pairs' game. Explain that one child in each pair is going to be a human recording machine who will 'play back' what the other one says. However, the playback takes place only when their partner has removed their finger from the imaginary pause button.

✦　　One child says aloud a sentence using familiar language and extends their index finger as if holding down a pause button.

✦　　The other child has to repeat the sentence that has been said but only when their partner releases their finger from the 'button'.

✦　　Suggest that on the first attempt, the 'button' is pressed for a short amount of time, eg five seconds, but increased on successive turns.

✦　　Don't forget to use this opportunity to discuss with the children the strategies they are using to memorize the sentence. This is a surprisingly challenging activity.

42. What am I saying?

✦ Mouth a sentence making sure all the children are in a position to see your face.

✦ Ask the children to guess what the sentence is.

✦ The importance of observing mouth shapes when learning a new language could be discussed.

43. Pictionary

By playing a version of this well-known game, the children will demonstrate that they can manipulate language in order to identify a sentence.

◆ Write familiar sentences on pieces of card, with a different sentence on each card, and arrange the class into groups.

◆ A child from each group picks up a card, reads the sentence silently and tries to convey the meaning by sketching on a piece of paper, without writing any words.

◆ The first child to correctly guess the sentence is the one to read the next card and do the sketch.

44. Freeze frame

✦ Read aloud a text already familiar to the children, such as a story, a list of instructions, a rhyme etc in the target language. You could allow the children to see the text as you read.

✦ At a suitable point, stop reading and ask the children to mime or perform an action for the last sentence you have read out.

45. Jumbled sentences

This could be played as a team game or with the whole class.

✦ Write sentences on a piece of paper and then cut them up so that each word is on a separate piece.

✦ An even better idea is to ask the children, in groups, to write a sentence using a choice of vocabulary. It may be necessary to check the accuracy of the sentence before the game begins.

✦ Give a cut-up sentence to each group and on a given signal ask the groups to work together and reconstruct the sentence.

✦ The first group to finish the task wins a point for their team.

46. Human sentences

This is quite a challenging activity.

✦ Use the pieces of paper from activity 45, 'Jumbled sentences' and give one piece to each child.

✦ Ask the children to circulate and try to find others who have words that could be used with theirs to create a sentence.

✦ Once these groups of children have been formed, suggest that they organize themselves into a line so that the words can be read from left to right, as appropriate. They should form a complete sentence.

✦ Invite each group, in turn, to read aloud their sentence, word by word. Ask the other groups to indicate whether or not they are correct.

✦ To familiarize the children with how the activity works, start with simple sentences and make them more complex as the children become more confident. This is particularly important if the sentence requires nouns, adjectives and verbs that must agree in gender.

47. Predict the sentence

This is one of the activities most requested by the children and one, surprisingly, that they are keen to play again and again in a lesson.

✦ Provide a written sentence building frame or scaffold from which the children can select a choice of familiar nouns, verbs, adjectives etc. The vocabulary should be presented to them in correct sentence order so there is no need to manipulate the words themselves.

✦ Distribute mini-whiteboards and pens, keeping one for yourself.

✦ Tell the children that you are going to select a noun, verb, adjective etc from the vocabulary scaffold and write a sentence on your whiteboard.

✦ Ask the children to do the same, telling them that the object of the game is to try to predict what you have written on your board.

✦ Ask the children to stand up when they have written their sentence and show it to you. This will give you an opportunity to give quick feedback on the accuracy of what they have written.

✦ Once everyone is standing, read your sentence out slowly. Depending on the structure of the target language, each word will probably indicate to the children whether they have the same sentence as you or not.

✦ Ask them to sit down if any word does not match yours. Those children who are still standing when you read the last word will have the same sentence as you and win a point.

✦   For a class of about 30 children, if you give them a choice of vocabulary to create about twenty possible sentences, the likelihood is that between one and three children will have the same sentence as you.

✦   The tension builds as each word and then each sentence is read out. This can continue until you think the game has to end owing to over-excitement. It may seem difficult to believe, but try it and see!

48. Unique sentence

This is a variation of activity 47, 'Predict the sentence' but equally popular. It requires the children to listen very carefully as well as giving them practice in reading aloud and writing.

✦ Present a vocabulary scaffold as before but this time tell each child that the objective is to try and write a sentence that no-one else will write.

✦ Ask all the children to stand up when their sentence is written. Each child reads out their sentence in turn from their mini whiteboard. Anyone with the same sentence raises their hand, sits down with the original author of the sentence and is out of the game.

✦ The children who are still standing once all the sentences have been read out, providing their sentences are correct, win a point each, as they have written a unique sentence.

✦ To ensure that a few children will have written unique sentences, there will need to be about three times as many possible sentences as children.

49. Mastermind sentence

✦ Once again, using a sentence scaffold, ask the children to work in pairs.

✦ Instruct each child to write down a sentence using the scaffolding, without allowing the other child to see what they have written.

✦ Each pupil takes it in turn to guess what their partner has written down by saying a sentence out loud. Their partner then indicates which words in the sentence were correct.

✦ The guesser notes them down. When it is their turn again, the guesser creates a sentence using the words they know to be correct along with other words to complete the sentence.

✦ Tell the children to take it in turns until one of them guesses the exact sentence written down by their partner.

50.   Pick a box

It is possible to purchase quite cheap, coloured stacking gift boxes which are useful for a variety of activities besides this one. Alternatively, use coloured shapes on an interactive whiteboard.

✦   Place a word in each coloured or numbered box, or behind each coloured or numbered shape. The words, when combined, will make sentences.

✦   Create two teams and choose someone from each team to take it in turns to pick a particular box or shape.

✦   If the word found is useful for the team's sentence, it is kept. If not, it is returned to the box, without allowing the other team to see what it is.

✦   The first team to create a sentence is the winner.

✦   A variation of this game is to allocate point numbers to each word. Once the sentence is completed the points are totalled and the winner is the team with the most points.

51. Running dictation

✦ Stick numbered pieces of paper with a sentence written on each one to the walls of the classroom, or even better, a large space such as the school hall.

✦ Divide the class into small teams and number each team according to the numbers of the pieces of paper on the walls of the room.

✦ Ask each team to elect a 'runner' who will go to their numbered piece of paper and memorize the sentence on it. This pupil will then return to their team and try to orally relay the sentence to them.

✦ Suggest that one child in the group is a 'scribe' who will note down the sentence using pencil and paper. Depending on the length of the sentence, the runner may need to shuttle several times between the wall and the scribe.

✦ The first team to write down the sentence correctly is the winner. Practice of the alphabet in the target language may be needed in order to spell the words correctly.

52. Invisible sentence

- ✦ Write a sentence on the board and ask the children to read it aloud.

- ✦ After each reading, remove one word from the sentence, not necessarily in the order in which it was written. Perhaps remove all the adjectives then all the nouns etc.

- ✦ Ask the class to read the sentence again, including the word or words that can no longer be seen.

- ✦ The removal of words continues until the class recites the whole sentence without the support of the written words.

53. Word substitution

This is a popular activity, as it involves standing at the front of the class. It is made even more appealing because these children can then be replaced by others.

- ✦ Use the word cards from activity 46, 'Human sentences' and distribute them to volunteers. They must then create a sentence by standing and holding the cards in the correct order.

- ✦ Distribute other cards, which could replace the nouns, adjectives, verbs etc in the sentence, to the pupils without cards.

- ✦ Ask the children, in turn, to replace a child in the line by standing in their place with their new word.

54. Longest sentence

Suggesting that children create something that is the longest or biggest etc, always seems to be an appealing challenge.

✦ Challenge pairs or groups of children to write the longest sentence they can and then read it aloud.

✦ Tell them it must be grammatically correct, including the punctuation. Provide a language scaffold with which to write the sentences.

55. Pass the parcel

This is similar to activity 9, 'Musical alphabet'.

✦ Arrange the children in a circle. Place a sentence, cut up into words, into a feely bag and play some music. Ask the children to pass the bag around the circle.

✦ When you stop the music, the child holding the bag removes a word and places it in the circle.

✦ When all the words have been removed and the music stops, the pupil holding the bag must arrange the cards to create a sentence.

56. Mismatch

✦ Create a list of sentence beginnings and a list of endings, which if put together, will not necessarily make sense but will be grammatically correct.

✦ Number the sentence starters and give a letter to the endings. Hide the sentence sections from view.

✦ Ask a child to select a number and letter and reveal the beginning and ending of the sentence.

✦ Ask the class to read the sentence aloud. It will most likely be an unusual combination, but the children will probably find it a humorous mismatch!

57. Question roll

✦ Divide the class into teams. Ask a question. The first person to answer correctly rolls a die.

✦ The number shown on the die is the number of points gained for that team. After an agreed number of rounds, the points are totalled.

58. Find the answer

✦   Give some children a card each with a question on it and some a card each with an answer on it.

✦   Ask the children with questions to circulate, asking their questions to children who are sat down holding answer cards.

✦   Once the response they receive matches their question, they also sit down until everyone has found their partner.

✦   If there are not enough questions for each child to have a different one, some of the questions and answers can be duplicated.

59.   Question and answer

This is similar to activity 58, 'Find the answer', except it involves only a few members of the class.

✦   Ask five or six volunteers to come to the front of the class. Hand a different question response card to each.

✦   Divide the class into two teams and distribute question cards to each team. A person from each team takes it in turns to name a classmate at the front and ask them a question. If the response matches the question, the team wins a point.

✦   Once an answer is correctly matched, the child standing at the front with that response sits down.

✦   If the children know a wide range of questions and answers, you may need to indicate possible questions to be used.

60.   Conversation jumble

✦   Ask for volunteers to stand at the front of the class and read aloud a sentence from a conversation.

✦   Arrange the children so that, as each child reads out their sentence, the conversation is jumbled up.

✦   Ask the other children to listen and then arrange the children in the correct order, so that when they read out their sentence, the conversation makes sense.

✦   This activity can also be played by writing the sentences on card and asking groups of children to arrange them in the correct order.

61. Roll a sentence

✦ Give the class a list of six pronouns, six verbs with endings that match the pronouns for a particular tense and six nouns. Each pronoun, verb and noun will be numbered one to six.

✦ One child takes a turn to roll three dice, preferably large foam dice so that everyone can see the number rolled.

✦ The number shown on the first die will select the pronoun, the second die the verb and the third die will select the noun.

✦ If the verb does not agree or the sentence does not make sense, the next child rolls the dice. If the sentence does make sense, it is written down and counts as one point.

✦ The child with the most correct sentences at the end is the winner.

Reading and decoding unfamiliar language

Children enjoy accessing authentic text, particularly if it gives them an insight into the lives of those from the country where the language is spoken. Access to non-fiction texts, songs, poetry and even fiction is possible through the use of the Internet. Sites for young children in the country of the target language also contain a wealth of suitable material. A pen friend link with a school in another country can provide hand-written resources. This gives the children an opportunity to experience the hand-writing style of the country where the target language is spoken. Finally, materials obtained on visits abroad can be sources of language for use in the classroom.

Activity 30, 'Splat the grapheme!'

62. Name that text

✦   To develop the skill of predicting meaning by identifying the context of language, provide the children with a selection of texts in different formats, such as recipes, news items, letters, weather forecasts etc.

✦   Name the formats from which text has been selected for the class and ask them to match the text to the format.

✦   Discuss the ways in which they came to their conclusions and suggest that children add their ideas to their 'language detective' notebooks.

63. Follow the instructions

Links to the cultural aspects of another country, such as food and dance, can provide opportunities for following instructions.

✦   Provide a set of instructions for a recipe or a simple dance with separate accompanying images.

✦   Ask the children to read and decode the text with the aid of a dictionary and match the images to each line of the instructions.

✦   Once they are familiar with the instructions, provide them with a version in which the sentences are cut up and ask them to rearrange them back into the correct order.

✦   If you're using a recipe, the dish could then be made under your guidance in a live demonstration.

✦ If you've used a dance, this could be taught by the children to younger learners.

✦ Alternatively, written instructions could be given to make a paper construction such as a fortune teller. The children could use dictionaries to write suitable messages.

64. Fill in the gaps

✦ Provide children with the lyrics of a song that has had some words removed. Then play it.

✦ Using a dictionary, ask the children to find the missing words.

✦ This is a very challenging activity and the words that have been removed should be carefully chosen, eg because they share a common sound or rhyming word.

✦ A simpler version of this would be to provide the missing words that require inserting.

65. Secret signal

This is a well-known activity for practising individual words. However, it could equally be used to practise reading text aloud.

✦ Ask a child to leave the room and agree with the rest of the class on a signal to be performed by another child, such as touching one's ear.

✦ The child outside then returns and the class starts to read aloud a section of text, say two or three sentences.

✦ When the selected child performs the secret signal, the class starts to read aloud from a different section of text.

✦ The change of text indicates to the child who went out of the room that someone has performed a secret signal. They must then try to guess who did it.

66. Quiz challenge

I designed a quiz, similar to that described below, for a 'foreign language day' to accommodate children who had completed an activity early. They could then work on the quiz while waiting for the rest of the class. It proved to be a very popular and engrossing activity.

✦ Create a series of questions in the target language, related to the language or culture of the country. Try to use structures with which the children are familiar but not necessarily familiar vocabulary.

✦ Put the children into small groups and provide bi-lingual dictionaries. The children then attempt to decode the question and work out the answer. If they give you the correct answer to a question, you provide them with a word in the target language.

✦ Once all the questions have been answered, the pupils will have several words. They must arrange these to make a sentence. The first group to discover the sentence is the winner.

Presentation, creativity and performance

Every act of communication can be considered a performance. Giving children opportunities to perform in front of others makes the communication meaningful. It is often not very difficult to find opportunities for this. Such opportunities could include:

✦ a performance to others in their class

✦ a performance of a story or rhyme for younger learners

✦ an assembly to the rest of the school and parents

✦ a video recording for a partner school

✦ a special performance for a foreign language day

✦ a performance for language teachers or students from the local secondary school.

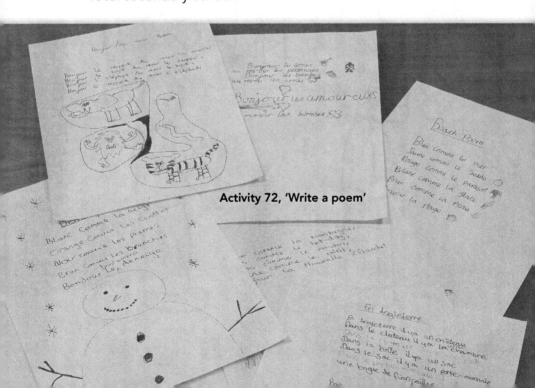

Activity 72, 'Write a poem'

67. Exclamation bean bag!

✦ Arrange the class in groups and give a bean bag to one child in each group.

✦ The child holding the bean bag names another child in the group and makes a statement before tossing the bean bag to the named child. The more surprising, shocking or unbelievable the statement, the better.

✦ The catcher responds with a suitable expression of shock, annoyance etc and then names the next child to catch the bean bag.

68. What am I describing?

✦ Ask the children to find a partner.

✦ Ask the class to describe an image to their partner from a selection presented on a page, or projected on a whiteboard. Make sure the images are all similar.

✦ The other child must try to identify which image is being described by asking for clarification as appropriate.

69. Recording stations

✦ If you have access to portable recorders, put children into small groups and ask them to write a sentence and record it.

✦ Place the recorders around the room and allow each group a limited amount of time at each recorder. They must listen to and write down the sentence.

✦ The sentences could be limited to a particular topic so that they are easier to identify, or they could describe images that are displayed.

70. Song contest

There are many commercially produced songs on CD for practising foreign languages. Use these as inspiration for children to write their own songs using familiar and unfamiliar language, with the help of a dictionary.

✦ You may want to suggest that the children use a familiar tune or rhyme as the basis for their song. Either suggest the topic or give them free range.

✦ Ask the children to write and practise their songs in small groups before performing them. This could be organized like a song contest, with the other groups voting, with a limited number of points, for each song.

✦ You may want to suggest that each group represents a country in the world where the target language is spoken.

71.   Be the teacher

This is an inspiring activity for the younger children being taught.

✦   Once your learners are very familiar with a particular song,
         rhyme or story, suggest that they teach it to other children,
         younger than themselves, in the school.

✦   Discuss what they will do to prepare for this. Suggest, for
         example, that they work in groups with different members
         being responsible for different parts of the story.

✦   Discuss ways in which the meaning of the performance will
         be understood, such as using actions, props and audience
         participation. This will give them an opportunity to reflect on
         their language learning strategies.

72.   Write a poem

Although, initially, many children doubt their ability to do this, they are often very surprised and pleased with their efforts on completion. It is important that you provide examples of simple poems on which the children can model their version. These can include:

✦   a colour poem on a particular theme: 'blue like the …', 'red like the…' etc

✦   a shape poem in which sentences are written in the shape of the object being described

✦   a hello/goodbye poem, eg 'hello sun, goodbye rain' etc

✦   a sequence poem in which prepositions are used to connect one object to another: 'in the house there is a cellar, in the cellar there is…'. This poem often catches their imagination.

The use of dictionaries will give them access to a wider vocabulary of unfamiliar words and structures, which allows them to be creative and inventive.

73.   Write a book

This sounds very challenging. However, if you choose a familiar story with repetitive language and allow access to a dictionary, it is possible for the children to substitute the original language with their own choices. They can then create their own version of the story; indeed, with the appropriate amount of support and structure, this can be a very engaging activity.

✦   The book could be hand written, word processed or in a PowerPoint presentation.

✦   Encourage the children to read their stories to younger learners.

74. Treasure hunt

✦ Arrange the children in small groups. Ask each group to select a small item from the classroom to act as 'treasure' and then agree on a hiding place.

✦ Ask the children to write clear and simple instructions in the target language so that another group can follow them and locate the treasure.

75. Invent a character

This activity works well in conjunction with a partner school in the target language country.

✦ Using a dictionary, ask the children to write a description of an imaginary alien, monster, character, animal etc.

✦ Send the descriptions to the partner school. If your school doesn't have one, they can be sent to another class or a neighbouring school.

✦ The recipients read the descriptions, draw the invented character and return this to the author.

76. Video presentation

✦ If you have access to a video recorder, you can ask the children to plan, film and present a video of their school.

✦ This could be sent to a partner school in the target language country, or another local school learning the same language.

✦ Discuss the content of the film and give the children access to a bi-lingual dictionary. The result could be a simple but useful presentation.

77. Who, what, where?

This results in varied and interesting role plays using a fixed amount of language.

✦ To practise a short conversation or role play, ask the children for suggestions as to who they might be, what they are doing and where.

✦ List these possibilities and ask the children to find a partner and choose from the lists.

✦ Ask the children to practise their conversations, changing responses appropriately according to their chosen character and situation.

Lightning Source UK Ltd.
Milton Keynes UK

172617UK00001BA/17/P